Channelling Childhood

Louise Berry (writing as l.e. berry) has had poems published in many anthologies – including Central Coast Poets anthologies, Blue Room Poets anthologies, Third Wednesday Poets anthologies and Poetry at the Pub anthologies – and in various issues of *Eucalypt*, *Women's Work*, *Margaret Olley poems*, *Food for Thought*, *Grevillea & Wonga Vine* and *To End all Wars*.

l.e. berry

Channelling Childhood

Acknowledgements

Poems in this collection which have been previously published are:
'Red Sandals', *Blue Room Poets* Volume II, 2016
an earlier version of 'Singleton', commended, *People of the Valley,* 2009
'My Teacher Said', *Blue Room Poets* Volume II
'Birthday Party', *Blue Room Poets* Volume II
'In my backyard', *Hunter* anthology, 2013

Channelling Childhood
ISBN 978 1 76041 827 4
Copyright © text l.e. berry 2019
Cover image: Judy Hooworth

First published 2019 by
GINNINDERRA PRESS
PO Box 3461 Port Adelaide 5015 Australia
www.ginninderrapress.com.au

Contents

Weekly Spelling Bee	7
English Class	8
Small Gifts	9
Judgements	10
Playground	11
Lines	13
School Holidays	15
Visiting Gran	17
Strangers In Our Midst	19
Country Roads	21
After the Art Gallery	22
Forbidden Fun	23
Birthday Party 1	24
Birthday Party 2	25
Separation	27
Wood For the Fire	29
Schooldays	30
North Sydney Pool	31
In My Backyard	32
Singleton	33
After the Blossom	35
If He Only Knew	37
Annual Outing	38
Balmoral	40
Hopscotch	42
Ocean	44
Hunter River	45
Inner Child	47
How Religion Stuffs Up Holidays, or Not	49
My Teacher Said	51

Not Fair	52
Going to School	53
One Morning	55
Primary Final	56
Red Sandals	57
Truth	60
Weekends	62
Fat Cat	63
Christmas Holidays	64
Lest I Forget	66
Scarlet	69
Learning	70

Weekly Spelling Bee

in wavy lines
like Noah's animals
we turn
face each other

wait

Miss yells out a word
first person spells
gets it right   she stays
gets it wrong   she sits

slowly the queues diminish
until only *that* Sarah Mills
stands opposite me
her lips curved in a sneer

Miss asks her to spell *believe*
she forgets
'i before e except after c'

I stand triumphant

Miss glares
   her pet faltered

I wait for
praise

wait

English Class

Sarah Mills smug   top of the class   this time   sure of her self-worth
Mum asks   *but is she nice*
I think *what's nice*   clammy hands leave marks   smudge my paper

   heat of effort
   imprint remains for others to follow
   or not

My knees shake   Miss Brown peers over steel-rimmed glasses purses her lips   takes an audible breath   sighs   I fear her next move

   anticipation
   brings needless pain
   pointless activity

My need to go   increases with pressure to perform   Mum said   *don't worry*   but   she's not here
she doesn't see the look on
Miss Brown's face   I want to be sick   bile burns my throat

   thought and body
   interact   not always in sync
   mind wins

Small Gifts

Miss says *pick up the papers*   inside I rebel   *they're not mine*

Miss says *do as I say*   Mum taught me to weigh the options
I say *what's an option*   Mum said   *if it's not worth the whack*
don't do it   I think   remember   pick up the papers

   experience
   governs our behaviour
   for a while

I shriek at Sally   *pick up*
what you dropped   Sarah sniggers   my face goes red
Sally pokes me
in the chest   *you're   not*
one   of   us
I kick her
I'm the one on detention

   life isn't
   a level playing field
   what's level

Helen Smith comes to class
her glasses   thicker than mine
Miss puts her next to me   I grin   smelly Martha flounces to
another desk   my nose is grateful   so am I

   small gifts
   arrive just in time
   like spring

Judgements

ding   dong

I run   think a friend
has come to play

Mum yells   *wait*
you never know who it is

what's wrong with grown-ups

worrying
about an unexpected
visitor

Playground

Sun's unrelenting heat
melts the bitumen

They cut the fig tree down
after Johnny fell and died

My feet burn
shoes stick at every step
squelch   smell

Mum doesn't understand
how tough life is
not like the olden days
when she was young

I wonder if I faint
will they release me from sport
allow me to sit in the cool

how can I make myself faint

Let me finish my book
live in an imaginary world
where kings and queens
are kind generous and brave

Some sweaty person yells
you're in
thrusts a bat at me
expects me to do something

I swing and miss
hope this ordeal is soon over
yet here comes another
accidentally I hit the ball

It heads for the trees
some do-gooder gives chase
oh no   they're going to
rescue it

My hand hurts
how can anyone enjoy this
they yell again
run   run   run

Look around
wondering where
my friend Helen points
I head in that direction

A bell sounds
humiliation comes to an end
but not recriminations
we could have won

Really
win this week
lose next
so…

Lines

i

children's laughter
wafts into the quiet

of a slave
writing lines

I shall not talk in class

ii

Mum's eyes narrow
as she waves a piece of paper
my knees shiver
anticipating
the cooking spoon

I search my conscience
but couldn't think
what she was on about now

the school says
you
are
disruptive in
class

I nearly smirk
trying to defend myself
they are so boring

Mum's eyes glint
how many times
have I
told you to behave

I close my eyes
try to recollect
something else so boring

my calves sting
apparently   she didn't want
an answer

I open my mouth
to protest

see my older brother
put his finger to his lips
shake his head

I swallow tears
remember being brave

School Holidays

i

time crept towards
school holidays

I didn't hate school
home's slightly better
though the younger ones drove
me bonkers

ii

I scanned the crowd
at the station
relieved to recognise my older brother

his godmother cast
her disapproving eye
over me

iii

at the foothills
the train's coal-fired engine
languished
the red carriage shuddered
as more grunt arrived
to push us up and over

iv

such fun

poking my head out the window
to get a face-full of soot

I chanted to myself
too sophisticated to say it aloud
I think I can   I think I can

as we rounded the mountain
children in the last carriage
waved   *hello*

Visiting Gran

i

Each Christmas
we journeyed to Sydney
stayed with Mum's parents

Gran had a Hills hoist
set in the slope of her lawn

We ran hard
swung free

Mum yelled
Gran admonished
Father tied it up

ii

We dug for potatoes
in the backyard
ate them for lunch

iii

Father grew carnations
loved Sims with their
skinny band of colour
Poppies with their hairy stems
and yellow centres
grew along the fence

iv

Mum told us about
poppy fields
the killing fields in Europe

About the red fields
of Flanders
where soldiers lay dead

How poppies made people
better   or remember
or   sometimes happy

I ate a poppy
felt sick
Mum gave me a whack
made me drink salt water

Strangers In Our Midst

i

you have to be polite
Mum admonished
these people have lost everything

we stared wide-eyed
as the woman came inside
a small girl clutched her hand

they spoke funny
the girl smelt funny
wore weird clothes

when Mum talked to them
they jabbered
in a foreign tongue called German

ii

on her way to the kitchen
Freida's corduroy trousers
scuffed against her thighs

she poured condensed milk
into hot tea
we drank the nectar
in the dawn light
before the household woke

iii

they stayed with us
for ever
the girl wouldn't play with me

you're too crude
I'm European
we are civilised

Gerta pinched me when Freida
wasn't looking
how civilised is that

I only tripped her up a little
she whimpered
such a sook

Mum broke the wooden spoon
on my legs

next time
I didn't confess

Country Roads

they said it was a treat   travel home by car not train   have a picnic on the way   my stomach tightened   in bilious anticipation I prayed today   things would be different   we swept around that fateful hill   car swayed and rocked   I reached for the towel   bile burnt my throat   I desired oblivion   to never feel like this again   *Don't worry*   *she'll get over it*   so glib of them   so unfeeling   I wanted to leave home   live in a world without twisting corners   where all the ground is flat

After the Art Gallery

no red dress
only certain women wear them

but…
no discussion

                               no consideration

in the haberdashery that afternoon
I felt the velvet
yielding and inviting like in the painting

Mum said earlier what a
beautiful woman
great colour in her face
pity she's a scarlet woman
old before her time

but…

one more word…

         I shrink inside

when I'm grown up I'll get a red dress

Forbidden Fun

pink feet
tiptoe down the stairs
run to the side door

small fingers struggle
to turn its handle

outside
still warm feet skip across the
icing on the grass

soft hands grab
the ancient green hose
slap it on the ground

my turn   my turn
our voices wake parents
time is running out

minute icebergs
quickly consumed

blue feet
run inside

find refuge in bed

Birthday Party 1

Coloured balloons float
Happy voices echo
Inside the hall
Lifting the gloom
Downpours created

Hunger satiated
Over fairy bread
Or occasional sausage roll
Downed in a hurry

Birthday Party 2

great excitement
off to the river for a picnic
my brother enjoys
privileges of his day

best sausage
right to blow out the candles
decide which game
to play

even to light sticks
under the grill
in a makeshift fireplace

Mum fixing a surprise
sends us away to play

Robin Hood
flavour of the month
we bicker to be Robin
who is Little John

staves in hand
we fight on the bank
slip into the river
get soaked

stay away from the river

we decide to look out for
the sheriff's men
climb the tree
hands shading our eyes

with a loud crack
my brother's branch
falls to the ground

I climb down
he looks very white
clutches his right arm

pack up we're going to the hospital

I thought we could eat the surprise
on the way

still hungry

Separation

i

parents yelling again

how come
they tell me to speak softly

I pull the pillow
over my head

dear God
please get them to stop
I'll be a good girl

in the morning
        no place set for Dad

Mum points
I go
upstairs to brush my teeth

Dad's toothbrush
        not there

my heart tightens
I sneak into Mum's bedroom

Dad's hairbrushes
        not there

I open the wardrobe

Dad's clothes
        not there

I drag my brother
to see
        Dad's stuff's gone

where's Dad

Mum says
he's gone away

ii

blue-green seas
yellow sand
jagged rocks
battered by time

childhood
summer holidays
no smog   no hassle
endless games

one day
car gone
then the picture
no longer on the wall

a month later
Dad gone
no explanation
never mentioned again

Wood For the Fire

with a groan and a struggle
the back gates opened wide

Mum bundled us away
behind closed doors

we raced each other up the stairs
looked outside to check the action

slowly Old Dobbin jerked inside
his driver fussed from side to side

slowly Old Dobbin inched forward
encouraged by his master's voice

with a rock and a groan
wood cascaded to the ground

the smell of sap and cut wood wafted
we raced downstairs to be the first

now don't climb it

we struggled to get to the top
slide down the crumbling pile

mum brandished a wooden spoon

if you don't get down you'll get this

worth the whack

Schooldays

the classroom is dim
I sniff
back tears

inner light
shines clear
through eyes
experienced
calm

elegant hands
clasp
my grubby
trembling ones

tell me again
calmly now
hitting another
not the way to go

North Sydney Pool

legs dangle over blue water
I watch people climb the tower
flex muscles and dive

my heart contracts
wondering   will I
ever find such courage

people seem so small
as their legs touch the bottom
then wriggle towards the surface

a stranger calls out
don't sit there go in   go on
I turn towards the voice

a hand in the small of my back
tumbles me into icy water
I struggle to catch breath

is this what drowning's like

I hit the bottom
flail around

my brother grabs my hand
pulls me to the surface
drags me to the edge

I dry retch
clamber onto solid ground

sob

In My Backyard

there's a swing
chains down each side
bolts
wooden seat

underneath
a dirt hollow
aligned
by dragging feet

on windy days
it swings by itself
to stop it
being lonely

Singleton

i

Aunt Vera yells
put your toys up
      the water's coming

silly old fool   what does she know
it never floods here

seven-year old wisdom
greater than any old person

we drag precious toys
from ground to table

the rain continues
no outside play   squabble inside

upstairs   go on

do I have to

do as you're told

yuk the toilets don't work

use a bucket

Mum wades
across the street

to get food

ii

lights flash as plane swoops
through trees

it's exciting to see the pilot
and coloured lights

iii

miners with black faces shovel
mud
with the carpet

too much

we're leaving

no fun
sent away to strangers

then to live
up a steep hill
in the city

it's safe from flood
Mum says

After the Blossom

cherries red-black and juicy
preserved in sugar
or coloured syrup
just the thing
for a summer morning

sitting on the veranda
spitting seeds
checking which goes the furthest
till Mum puts a stop to fun

having contests to see
who can be the first
to eat the flesh
leave the stone
on the stem

but then
someone drops one
it rolls away unseen

until

in the dead of night
heading for a midnight snack
it squashes underfoot
slides the foot away
hand grabs a chair

*what do you think you're doing
making such a racket*

nothing Mum – thought I heard a mouse

rearrange the chair
cover
hide the stain
creep back to bed

If He Only Knew

Uncle Tony
always said
he grew
my little sister's first curl

pity he didn't grow her personality

she always said
I'm special
he grew my curl
not yours

grrr...

if only she knew
my hate of
curls
so girly
so belittling

it's a curly question
whether to tell her
or not

decisions   decisions   decisions

Annual Outing

I have this funny feeling
in my stomach
it's butterflies
I don't know how they got in

Gran drives the green car
onto the road
let's me sit up front
like an adult

we go to town
Christmas time
David Jones is full
of tinsel and carols

the man in the lift
calls out the floors
and what's on them
children's wear

Gran and I
walk towards
rows of dresses
clustered on racks

a woman in black
smiles at Gran
calls her madam
I giggle

Gran frowns
I squirm
hope I will still get
a Christmas dress

my heart stops
she pulls out one
with a square neckline
Cinderella's coach around the hemline

Gran keeps searching
my eyes stray back
to that wonderful dress
Gran looks at me

we'll try that one on
I skip after the woman
into a small room
take off my old dress

my eyes sparkle
I feel like a princess
it fits me
no need for alterations

Gran smiles
I smile
sad as I take it off
grin as I carry the bag

Balmoral

it had been a long day
Mum sat there
book in hand
occasionally looking up

my brother and I
had to care for
the younger ones
again

why don't I get a turn
to just be me
swim by myself
lie on my back

if only I were an orphan
then it would be quiet
no one to tug my hand
my turn   my turn

I grab the child
swing her high
let her go
she falls into the water

that wasn't nice
my brother   my conscience
I shrug
my sister wails

I feel guilty
again
come on let's do it again
a trusting hand grabs mine

the afternoon continues

Hopscotch

chalked squares
line the pavement
outside my home

I find my tor
it's smooth and oval
discovered at the beach

a friend joins
gaggle of siblings
lining up for their turn

we toss our tors
to see which goes
the furthest

winner gets first go
so
we squabble over

how close to the line
anyone stood
before throwing

as we start
wind whips up
blows a throw off course

to the delight of those
waiting impatiently
for their turn

the game progresses
amid yells   screams
and laughter

no quarter given
to those with
shorter legs

the rules are the rules

daylight fades
as we hop
struggle for balance

leap from square
to square
check we missed the lines

heated discussion
history retold
about smudged lines

game ends
the older ones
win as usual

satisfied
we troop inside
milk and biscuits

Ocean

flecks of white
like a magic rope
run along the swelling waves
seaweed escapes the sand

small footsteps falter
toes scrunch up
feet retreat
from the sticky foam

wind blows hard
sprays sand
stings bathers
empties the beach

from inside the car I see
the exhausted ocean calms

wind dies down
seagulls screech
waves roll in then retreat

Mum takes us home

Hunter River

at our special place
there is a big tree
a rope
a fallen branch

my brother shows
what to do
first run along the log
grab the rope and swing free

what if I fall

I peer down at the water
see it ripple over rocks
hesitate

grow up   swing out wide into the calm

I shiver
scared about my rite of passage

you want some cheese

I glare
how dare he mock me
I am brave

I take a deep breath
run
grab the rope
and a prayer

cool water swirls
I sink deep into the quiet pool
feel grown-up
no longer a child

the river bank seems so far away
I swim   tread water   swim
scramble through the mud
reach solid wood

well done

I find the strength to smile

Inner Child

I want to play
feel wind in my hair
splash in the pool
not visit boring Aunt Mary

>*I told you before*
>*duty before pleasure*
>*your character needs building*
>*prepare for the future*

but this is now
I want what I want
things change all the time
I yearn to be free

>*don't be selfish*
>*you need discipline*
>*your aunt is kind*
>*do as I say*

I won't be tied down
told what to do
I'll make my decisions
live my own life

>*we can visit the zoo*
>*on our way home*
>*ride the elephant*
>*roar at the lions*

hurry up hurry
it's time we were going
my aunt is waiting
there's no time to waste

How Religion Stuffs Up Holidays, or Not

i

Mum   Mum   when are we going

> God comes first,
> once we've been to church

do we have to
doesn't he say ask and you shall receive
so I've asked   can we go now

> it doesn't work that way
> you have to put in the effort first
> then hope he'll look after you

Mum, Mum

> I hope you're packed
> we can leave from church

Mum, Mum
Beth's got my book
and won't give it back

> don't forget God's watching
>
> you do want
> a great holiday
>
> remember to be
> nice to each other

but Mum

> enough

ii

the road snakes ahead
almost still cars
a lengthy ribbon

what's going on
why aren't we moving

>   keep quiet
>   be thankful I made
>   you go to church
>
>   or you might be
>   lying dead
>   because a truck lost its load

My Teacher Said

my teacher said
>*pick up the papers*

my heart rebelled
>they're not mine

my teacher said
>*line up, girls*

she sent the cane down with a
whack onto my palm

my teacher said
>*girls, you need to do your best*
>*be kind and generous*

>what about her

my teacher said
>*you'll be rewarded in heaven*
>*for your hard work*

>what about in hell

my teacher said

I can't recall
by now I tuned out to her words
listened only to the tone

my mother said
>*there's no rest for the wicked*

I wonder if that's why
my teacher ran around a lot

Not Fair

Robert Dickerson an important artist
painted people
dark lines around their faces

Mum showed me in a book
how Ronald Searle drew

knew what to do
when told to draw the Last Supper

tongue between my teeth
outlined faces in black
and their bodies too

I overheard Mum say
to my teacher
oh dear – not an artistic bone in her body

held my breath
hoping for support

my teacher said
she is a serious girl

defeated   deflated
believed I had no talents

Going to School

i

Mum said
it's not far
I don't understand why you take so long

I looked at my brother
he glared at me

Mum said
Just get to school on time

ii

suitcases in hand
we walked down the lane
looked both ways
crossed to the paddock

come on don't dawdle
I sniffed at the injustice
I don't

I saw my brother stop
bend down pick up something

my chubby legs ran as fast
as a speeding train

what's that?

he held out his hand
clutching a small lizard

it bit me
I ran away screaming

my brother caught my arm

stop it
everyone will hear
and…

I gulped
holding my hand

show me

I held my hand out
he groaned

what a fuss over nothing
see

I looked but couldn't find
any blood

the school bells were ringing
as we ran through the gates

One Morning

Mum always said
>*don't talk to strangers*

she said
>*don't dawdle*
>*get to school on time*
>*you were late yesterday*

we went a new way
to school
past the oval
no games for us today

we were being good
hurrying until
a voice under a hat
called us by name

we ran as fast as we could
I tripped
hurt my knee
hobbled the rest of the way

we got there just as the bell was ringing

Mum said
>*Mrs Green is a friend of mine*
>*you weren't very polite*
>*running away like that*

I thought she was a witch
wanting to cook us

Primary Final

i

under the peppercorn tree
I mimicked university students
studying for exams

the raucous song
of Black Princes and Green Grocers
lulled me into sleep

the book falling
onto my big toe
brought me back to life

ii

anxiously I scanned the paper
my heart thumped
my name was there
an 'H' beside it

what does that mean
my mother smiled slyly at me
helped

my heart dropped
I fought back tears

what's wrong with you

it's a joke

you're too sensitive

Red Sandals

i

within a large family
I feel lost
not sure of my worth
other than as mother's little helper

the pressure of being a big sister
saps my sense of me
school teaches me about martyrs
gives me a fresh identity

ii

Gran's Austin A40
weaves the twisting highway
then pauses by the roadside
while I throw up

iii

on the train   sights and sounds
catch my attention
reveal the divide
between city and country

iv

each window holds fairy-tale scenes
just like in the books
tinsel and glitter dangle
from counters and ceilings

the liftman calls out the floors
his empty sleeve folded neatly
Gran tells me not to stare
ladies are more polite

on the way to the children's section
a pair of red sandals
just like in the film
beckons me

Gran is going past
my mind says to follow
yet my heart wills me
to stop and stare

v

I am Dorothy
capable of sending me
away from this life
whenever I click my red heels

vi

red sandals flash
as I run
my heart sings
I am me   I am free

vii

day and night
relentless rain
until streets
are swollen rivers

water invades our home
sweeps away
the red shoes
my sense of me

viii

at school
I tell of my loss
tear streaked face
sorrow too big to conceal

Mum whacks me
you said what

*our loss is so much greater
than just your shoes*

Truth

Mum instils the need for truth
she says

> *if you want to tell me a lie*
> *tell me a clever one*
> *but there are no clever lies*

yet

I was walking along the corridor
a class mate walked by
I said

you smell of the stables

she raced after me
whacked me with a wet mop
right in the back
of my lemon uniform

Mum said
> *you were impolite and hurtful*

I protested *I told the truth*
That's what you said I must do
she said
> *there's no excuse for rudeness*

parents

she made me wear the uniform
with its spider on the back
every week
all year

this'll teach you
*   to behave*

it taught me
Mum wasn't always right

Weekends

driven to Balmoral
swim around boats
sprinkle salt
onto potato crisps

taking the Manly ferry
seasick
cling to the wire
think I will die

swim at the beach
see Norfolk pines
walk along the Esplanade
feel the holiday mood

travel to the zoo
looking over the harbour
watch big elephants
gape at giraffes' blue tongues

catch train to Singleton
put head through window
get covered in soot
smell coal burn

get carsick
throw up everywhere
depressed
isolated

do it all again

Fat Cat

his beard gleamed white
he turned his head
disappearing into the night

sleek   lithe   randy
he courted far and wide
enjoyed himself under Mum's window

enough
she took him to the vet
brought home an It who

>	no longer preened
>	in front of the television
>
>	no longer sought affection
>	from home
>	or abroad

his once blinding beard
turned a dusty shade of grey
matching his lustreless coat

he entertained himself
waddling down the hall
until a wall stopped his journey

he shook his head
repeated his journey

Christmas Holidays

i

great excitement
Father is taking us
into town to see *War and Peace*

the little ones have
to stay at home
too gory for them Mum said

ii

our eyes grew wide
Napoleon strutted one hand in his coat
the other behind his back

snow did not stop him
he rotated his hat across his head
left his eyes free

iii

after the battle
Pierre drowns his sorrows
perched in the window
high above the snow

iv

we show younger siblings
how to stand on the veranda railing
lean back   sway

grasp a bottle of water
raise it in the air yell *freedom*
lean back and drink

v

Mum was a spoilsport
gave us a whack said we were a disgrace
forbade us on the railing

vi

we had to be content
to strut around hands in our coats
hats on sideways

making swords
tied with strips from Mum's tree
with the purple flowers

she said we were vandals
with no knife how else
could we make the swords

it wasn't our fault

Lest I Forget

those dark days of childhood
        dread in my heart
Anzac Day was coming

Dad died TPI
left a legacy of young Australians
to struggle on alone

we were allowed to call him Don
        the stranger who needed
        a home
shot down over the ocean
rescued by his childhood friend
Peter the persuader

Don was a large dark man
dark of hair   complexion
thought   speech and   views
his aura reflective of his beard
his bitter sense of humour
his twisted view of life
his endless rum-drinking

from a barrel of a chest
gorilla arms
accompanied by sarcastic jokes
would lift and move his legs
creaking the wheelchair

preparations made for endless visitors
as Anzac Day approached
I hinted to my mother
my anxiety about the day
I'm rebuffed as being selfish

this is the one day just the one day
I can talk about the war
no one who hasn't been there
could possibly understand

that morning spent
listening to the march
endless stories of bravery
sacrifice   boredom
my younger siblings restless
wanting to go outside to play

tension in the house increased
when Peter came around
I didn't understand then
obligations imposed
by saving someone's life

bitterness of survival
an endless burden
saviour bewildered
the rescued preferred death
to a dependent life

as the day dragged into night
voices in the room rose
sounds of flesh on flesh
would issue from the gloom

in bed
blankets over my head
I weep for me
my childhood and them

Scarlet

drip drip drip
splatters of red
splotch the pristine white
of the basin

if I ever wondered
how far liquid went
then I need no longer

a teaspoonful is enough
to leave its mark
anywhere

get over it

I blindly grab more tissues
ineffectually dab
the bloody mess

if only I were
blue-blooded like Princess Anne

Learning

teenage years
opened my eyes
to many things

        wisdom

parents' hang-ups
passed onto
offspring

        alas

taught to dress
beneath
cotton nightgowns

        shame

pleasure
in having a body
or sensations
        forgotten

if I had known
the delight
another could give

        I'd have grown up earlier

www.ingramcontent.com/pod-product-compliance
Lightning Source LLC
Chambersburg PA
CBHW062154100526
44589CB00014B/1833